ZECHARIAH

ZECHARIAH

Stephen Kaung

Christian Fellowship Publishers, Inc.
New York

Paperback ISBN: 978-1-68062-142-6
Hardcover ISBN: 978-1-68062-157-0
eBook ISBN: 978-1-68062-143-3

Available from the Publishers at:

11515 Allecingie Parkway
Richmond, Virginia 23235
www.c-f-p.com

Printed in the United States of America

Preface

Zechariah's prophesying began with a call for the remnant of the children of Israel to return to Him: "Return unto me, ... and I will return unto you" (1:3b). They had already returned physically, but their hearts needed to be recovered. Thank God they responded and returned with their whole hearts. The result was that the Lord returned to them as well.

After about two months, the word of God came to Zechariah in one busy night, with eight consecutive visions, each added to the other. Through these visions, God made known His whole plan of recovery. It was not just to recover the temple that Zerubbabel and Joshua and the remnant were building, but at the very end of days, He would recover everything to its fullest. Through these visions, we can see the whole plan of God in the work of recovery. In the end, God is going to recover fully and gain glory out of His people.

In this volume, Stephen Kaung brings us through this same path of returning to the Lord with our whole hearts. He then seeks out the prophetic word of the Lord through Zechariah in our time.

May the Lord use these words to comfort and encourage today's struggling remnant. May we not despise "the day of small things." It is "not by might, nor by power, but by [His] Spirit" that the church is built.

Contents

Note

The author delivered this series of messages in February 1974, before a group of Christians gathered for worship in Richmond, VA. The texts of these messages were recorded and later transcribed. Some portions of the recordings were missing and filled in using the author's preparatory notes. These notes also included several gold nuggets missing in the messages but now included in this volume.

Unless otherwise indicated,
Scripture quotations are from the
New Translation by J. N. Darby.

1—Zechariah the Prophet

Zechariah 1:1—In the eighth month, in the second year of Darius, came the word of Jehovah unto Zechariah the prophet, the son of Berechiah, the son of Iddo ...

In the Old Testament, the return of the remnant of the Jews from captivity typifies the recovery of the testimony of God. Ezra and Nehemiah give us the background stories of this remnant of Israel. There are three prophetic books connected with the two historical books: Haggai, Zechariah, and Malachi. These, too, are closely related to the history of recovering the testimony of God.

The Recovery of the Testimony of God

The remnant of Israel returned from Babylon to Jerusalem to rebuild the house of God and later on to rebuild the wall of the city. The testimony of God was restored on the earth through these two experiences of rebuilding both the house of God and the wall of the city.

Today, as well, the Lord is doing the work of recovery. He is recovering the testimony of Jesus on this earth through His people, the church. But for the testimony of Jesus to be recovered, two things have to be restored. First, is the rebuilding of His house—which is our lives together with God. We, "as living stones, are being built up a spiritual house, a holy priesthood, to offer spiritual sacrifices acceptable to God by Jesus Christ" (I Peter 2:5). This must be restored. We not only need for our individual lives with God to be restored, but also our corporate life together with God, as His house, as a people who worship, who serve Him, who satisfy His heart. This must be recovered and restored among God's people.

Second, is the rebuilding of the walls of Jerusalem—which is our love for one another, our being built up together as one. "Behold, how good and how pleasant it is for brethren to dwell together in unity!" (Psalm 133:1) This must be restored so that we may truly be a testimony to this world that we are one.

Haggai and Zechariah

Haggai's name means festive or festival. Most likely he was an old man. He saw the temple built by Solomon and destroyed by Babylon. In his old age God raised him up as a prophet to speak for God. God used him to touch the conscience of the remnant and urged them to "consider [their] ways" before God.

How could they build their own houses and leave the house of God in ruins? They said things like, "This is not the time to build the house of God." So God said, "Is it time for you to build your own houses? Consider your ways. Why is it that you are so frustrated? Why is it that you are never satisfied? Why is it that you sow much and reap little? You eat much but you are still hungry. You drink and you are not satisfied. You are clothed but you never get the warmth from it. You earn wages but the wages fall into a bag with holes." Why was this their situation? Because their priority was wrong. "But seek ye first the kingdom of God and his righteousness, and all these things shall be added unto you" (Matthew 6:33). If the order is reversed, nothing will be satisfying. Thank God for the prophetic ministry of Haggai! Through his ministry, the remnant rose up as one man to put their hands to the work of rebuilding the house of God.

In the eighth month, in the second year of Darius

Haggai started to prophesy in the sixth month of the second year of King Darius (see Haggai 1:1). As an old man, Haggai spoke very little. He only spoke a few times and very briefly. The whole period of his prophecy lasted only about four months. And yet the impact upon the remnant was tremendous.

Then in the eighth month, after Haggai's ministry was fulfilled, God raised up the young man Zechariah. The Bible says that by the testimony of two or three, everything shall be established (see Deuteronomy 19:15). God not only raised up Haggai as His prophet but also raised up Zechariah to confirm and establish the testimony. By the witnessing of two—and later on, three with Malachi—every word of God was established.

The wonderful thing was that God raised up an old man to be His prophet, who was probably in his nineties. And then God raised up a young man. We do not know exactly how young Zechariah was, but probably he was in his early twenties. God combined these two men to help, encourage, and strengthen the hands of the remnant in the rebuilding of the house. There was no generational gap here. The old and the young were together as one in the work of God.

How do we know that Zechariah was a young man? In Zechariah 2, the Lord said, "Run, speak to this young man, saying …" (v.4). If he was a young man when he started to prophesy, he was likely just a kid when Zerubbabel and Joshua returned from captivity. He may have returned to Jerusalem from Babylon with his grandfather when he was just a lad. Some people even think that he was just an infant when he returned.

the son of Berechiah, the son of Iddo

Sometimes Zechariah was called the son of Iddo. Sometimes he was called the son of Berechiah. Why? Most probably, his real father, Berechiah, died while he was young so he was brought up by his grandfather Iddo. According to the Jewish way of speaking, he may also be called the son of Iddo.

We learn from Nehemiah 12 that Iddo was a Levite, a priest (see vv. 1, 4). So Zechariah came from a priestly family and would have served in the temple after it was built. But before he ministered in the temple as a priest, God called him to be a prophet while he was yet a young man.

How is it that God raised up this young man as a prophet? We would think it would take an old man to be a prophet because an old man would be mature. He would have all those long years behind him and many experiences before God. Surely God can use such a mature person, but how could God use a young man as a prophet? We learn that God has no respect for age. As long as God could find a heart after himself, He will use him.

At the Foundation of the Second Temple

This old man, Haggai, had seen the old temple built by Solomon. When he saw the temple was in ruins and was delayed in being built, he must have labored before God. There must have been "the travail of his soul." There must have been much prayer from this prophet asking God to revive the heart of the remnant so that they might return to the rebuilding work. His heart was so exercised before God that God called him to be His mouthpiece.

The same principle happened with this young man, although he had never seen the temple built by

Solomon. He did not look back to that because he had not seen Solomon's Temple. Instead, he was a young lad as he returned, full of hope that there would be a new temple as a testimony of God on earth. When he saw that the older people—like his father, his uncles, and those of the older generation—were busily occupied with building their own houses, leaving the house of God in ruins, this young lad was exercised before God. He did not look back, but he did look forward. As he looked forward, he was concerned that the temple should be built.

I wonder if, as a lad, he was among those young ones when the foundation of the temple was laid. The second year after the remnant came back, they laid the foundation of the house. When the foundation was laid, the old men wept. They had seen the temple built by Solomon, and now that they saw the foundation laid, they wept with joy. When the young ones that had never seen the temple built by Solomon saw the foundation laid, they shouted with joy. I wonder if this lad was among those who shouted. Young men can certainly get carried away by enthusiasm. He must have been one of the little kids jumping around and shouting and praising, knowing that now the foundation was laid. There was nothing wrong with that.

After the foundation was laid, nothing was built upon it. This young lad must have grown up wondering what happened. He had a life with God that was not superficial. He must have been exercised before God, looking for the Second Temple to be built.

Similar to Jeremiah

In many ways, Zechariah was like another prophet, Jeremiah. Jeremiah was called by God when he was young as well.

> And the word of Jehovah came unto me, saying, Before I formed thee in the belly I knew thee; and before thou camest forth out of the womb I hallowed thee, I appointed thee a prophet unto the nations. And I said, Alas, Lord Jehovah! behold, I cannot speak; for I am a child. But Jehovah said unto me, Say not, I am a child; for thou shalt go to whomsoever I shall send thee, and whatsoever I command thee thou shalt speak (Jeremiah 1:4-7).

When the call of God came to him, Jeremiah said, "Who am I? I am but a boy, a young man. How can I be Your mouthpiece?" Jeremiah was called while he was young just as Zechariah was. He too came from a priestly family. He was a priest, but he was also a prophet, just as Zechariah was from a priestly family and a prophet. Jeremiah lived during the time of the end of the nation of Judah. This was before the Babylonian captivity and a little during the captivity. In view of what was going to happen he warned the people. He called the people to repentance, and his heart went out and he wept. He was known as the weeping prophet.

But Zechariah lived during the time of recovery. He looked forward with hope to see the temple restored. Shall we say he was a laughing prophet? He was a prophet of hope, not of despair. And his hope, of course, was in God. This is the only place where you can put your hope. Don't put your hope in yourself; you will be disappointed. Don't put your hope in man; you will be disappointed. But if we put our hope in God, He will not disappoint us.

So, Zechariah was sometimes called the prophet of hope. Being a young man, he was a young man full of imagination. And dare I say, if your imaginations are sanctified, God can use them. Haggai, as an old man, spoke very briefly; but Zechariah saw visions. He spoke many words, but they were sanctified.

Similar to John the Apostle

Zechariah was also like another young man, this time from the New Testament—John, the apostle. John was so intense and utter before the Lord. He knew nothing of a compromised or in-between life. To him, there was no such thing as a gray area. Everything was either black or white. With John, it was always an absolute devotion to God.

He also always went back to the beginning and looked forward to the ultimate, the consummation.

That was John. If you read his Gospel, his Epistles, and the Revelation, you will realize this. There was no compromise. He was utter for the Lord.

John was also a man full of visions and imagination. Through John, God gave us the Apocalypse, the book of Revelation in the New Testament. Some people say that through Zechariah, God gave us the apocalypse of the Old Testament. These two young men were very similar.

Zechariah the prophet was a young man whose heart was towards the Lord. He was interested and occupied in the things of God. He was full of burden with the concern of God. The Lord found one who had a heart after God, and He began to use him greatly in the work of recovery.

2—Recovery of the Heart

Zechariah 1:1-3—In the eighth month, in the second year of Darius, came the word of Jehovah unto Zechariah the prophet, the son of Berechiah, the son of Iddo, saying, Jehovah hath been very wroth with your fathers. And thou shalt say unto them, Thus saith Jehovah of hosts: Return unto me, saith Jehovah of hosts, and I will return unto you, saith Jehovah of hosts.

Haggai started to prophesy in the sixth month of the second year of King Darius (see Haggai 1:1). Through his prophesying, Zerubbabel, Joshua, and the remnant were quickened in their spirits, and they rose up to build. By the end of the sixth month, they began rebuilding the temple.

In the seventh month—after a month of their laboring on the rebuilding of the temple—the word of God came to Haggai again to encourage them (see Haggai 2:1). He told them not to despise what they were doing because the "latter glory of this house shall be greater than the former." Haggai continued to prophesy to them. He even prophesied about the day when the Messiah would come.

In the eighth month,
in the second year of Darius

Then in the eighth month, Zechariah came in to prophesy. Why do I mention these dates? Because these are important for us to understand the situation for Zechariah's prophecy.

Back in the sixth month, as Haggai began to prophesy, the remnant listened to the voice of God. They started to build. When it came to the eighth month, as Zechariah began to prophesy, they had already been working on the temple for over a month. Just think, this young man whose heart was with the Lord, who was concerned about the rebuilding of the temple, had now seen the remnant work on it for over a month. What will he feel at that time? He would certainly be rejoicing before the Lord. "People have started to rebuild the temple! Isn't that marvelous? The Lord has answered my prayers. The Lord is beginning to do a marvelous work with His people!"

This young man must have felt very happy as he saw these people working on the temple. But Zechariah was not a superficial young man. Though he may at first feel happy as the people began to work on the temple, he was still before the Lord. As he waited before the Lord, the Lord revealed something to him. When the revelation came to him, he started to prophesy. What was the message of the Lord for these people who came back from Babylon? What was the message of God for those who started the work and now resumed the building of the temple? It was a surprising word.

Return unto me, saith Jehovah of hosts, and I will return unto you

We might expect a message of the Lord to such a people would be: "I am very happy and satisfied with you." On the contrary, the word of the Lord that came to Zechariah was: "Return unto me ... and I will return unto you." Isn't that strange? If this word was spoken to those who remained in Babylon, it would seem fitting. If this word was spoken to the remnant who returned to Jerusalem but did not work on the temple, that would also seem to be all right. But here was a remnant who had left Babylon, been uprooted from everything for the sake of God, came back to Jerusalem, and now labored in the building of the house of God. Yet the word of God came to them saying, "Return unto me."

Had they not already returned? Yes, they returned. They were not in Babylon; they were in Jerusalem. Had they not returned to do the work? Yes, they had returned to build the house of God, and their hands were busy building. Yet the word of God to His people was, "Return unto me." It was as if they still needed to return. Think of that!

You know, our God is a most thorough God. When He deals with us, He deals with us with such thoroughness. He will not leave any stone unturned.

When He begins His work with us, He will see that it is done to the utmost.

He wanted the people to come out of Babylon to return to Jerusalem. He wanted His people to come out of confusion and return to simplicity—out of the complexity of this world, returning to the simplicity that is in Christ. Of course, He wanted to do that.

He also called them to rebuild His house. In the same way, He calls us to rebuild that we may be built up together as His house to offer spiritual sacrifices to Him. But He wants more.

You may return to Jerusalem to a position, you may put your hand to build the temple doing a work, but have you returned to *Him* as a Person? He is more interested in your relationship with Him than your relationship with a work or your relationship with a position. The position is correct, the work is right, but He himself is more important than everything else. And He will never be satisfied until He knows that you have returned to *Him*. That is what He wants.

I have found something very strange that happens whenever you turn to God. It seems as if *before* you turn to God, He is gentle with you, but the moment you *begin* to turn to God, His hand immediately begins to be heavy upon you. It is strange. There are many things He will not say to you if you are far away from Him. But as you come back to Him, He will begin to speak to you about them. It is very strange. Why is it this way?

Because He wants you; because He loves you; because He wants to have you completely. He wants your heart.

The remnant had resumed the work of rebuilding the temple. Everything looked fine outwardly. But God looked upon their hearts.

> For the eyes of Jehovah run to and fro through the whole earth, to shew himself strong in the behalf of those whose heart is perfect toward him (II Chronicles 16:9a).

They did have a heart for the Lord, or otherwise, they would not have returned. They had a heart for the Lord, or else they would not be doing the work of rebuilding. But God saw their heart was not fully toward Him, and because of that, God was not satisfied.

God said, "Return unto me. Return unto me with a perfect heart. Do not be too much concerned about the work in your hands." Now, that is what they were concerned with. They were thinking, "Now we are building this house, but it can never match up with the temple built by Solomon. Oh, this is just a small thing!" They were very much concerned with their work. So God said, "Don't be concerned with your work; it is *My* work. Be concerned with your heart. If your heart returns to Me, I will return to you. There is no problem with the work. Return unto Me, and I will return unto you."

Thus saith Jehovah of hosts

In one short verse, the phrase "saith the Lord of hosts" occurs three times. Does this strike you?

> And thou shalt say unto them,
> **Thus saith Jehovah of hosts**:
> Return unto me,
> **saith Jehovah of hosts**,
> and I will return unto you,
> **saith Jehovah of hosts**
> (Zechariah 1:3 **emphasis** added).

Three times the Lord repeats this phrase "saith the Lord of hosts." Why? This message was so emphatic. He did not want people to miss it. They may miss it thinking they are all right. The Lord said, "No, it is not all right. You have to return, return unto Me, and I will return unto you."

The people were wondering whether the Lord would return unto them, whether the Lord would begin to bless them. Though they had labored on the temple for over a month, the drought was still there. The blessing of the Lord through rain did not come. They were wondering whether the blessing would ever come. But the prophet said, "Do not worry about that. You do not need to fear that. Return unto Me, because it is a matter of your heart. Return with a perfect heart that knows nothing but God himself, and He will take care of everything else."

Oh, brothers and sisters, how complicated we are. We are concerned with this, troubled with that, thinking of this, feeling insecure about that, and wondering and puzzling about things all the time. There is a simplicity in Christ. Just return to the Lord with your whole heart, and He will take care of the matter. That is the way.

Have we today responded to the Lord by coming out of the complexity of this world? Are we now standing on the ground of the simplicity of Christ? Have we been stirred by His Spirit, as it were, to lay our hands on the building of the house of God? If so, remember that the Lord looks beyond these things. There is a word for us from the Lord. It is especially for those who have returned, who are building the house of God. That word is, "Return unto me—saith the Lord of hosts—and I will return unto you."

Be ye not as your fathers

Then the prophet used the former generation, before the captivity, as an illustration.

> Be ye not as your fathers, unto whom the former prophets cried, saying, Thus saith Jehovah of hosts: Turn ye now from your evil ways, and from your evil doings; but they did not hearken nor attend unto me, saith Jehovah. Your fathers, where are they? and the prophets, do they live for ever? But my words and my statutes, which I commanded my servants the prophets, did they not overtake your fathers? And they

turned and said, Like as Jehovah of hosts thought
to do unto us, according to our ways and
according to our doings, so hath he dealt with us
(Zechariah 1:4-6).

The children of Israel had been in captivity for
seventy years. By the time Zechariah prophesied, almost
a century had passed. And now, the Lord turned their
attention back to the days before the captivity. God said,
"Do you notice your fathers? They did not listen to Me.
They would not return to Me. I sent prophets to them,
and yet they would not listen to the voice of the
prophets."

Do you remember who those prophets were? God
sent prophets such as Jeremiah, Amos, and Hosea. They
warned the children of Israel, begging them to return to
God. They would not listen. These forefathers were
gone. Even the prophets did not live forever. They were
gone. But the word of God and His statues remain
forever. They still stand. Every word of God is fulfilled
but may be fulfilled in a tragic way.

God said, "Do not be like your fathers, do not
harden your hearts. Listen to the voice of the prophets
and return completely unto God." This is the message
God had spoken through Zechariah—return unto Me.

God is never satisfied just by our rebuilding work.
God looks into our hearts. He desires a perfect heart
that is toward Him. This alone will satisfy Him and
nothing else.

3—The First Vision: Jealousy

Zechariah 1:7-17—Upon the four and twentieth day of the eleventh month, which is the month Shebat, in the second year of Darius, came the word of Jehovah unto Zechariah the prophet, the son of Berechiah, the son of Iddo, saying, I saw by night, and behold, a man riding upon a red horse, and he stood among the myrtle-trees that were in the low valley; and behind him were red, bay, and white horses. And I said, My lord, what are these? And the angel that talked with me said unto me, I will shew thee what these are. And the man that stood among the myrtle-trees answered and said, These are they whom Jehovah hath sent to walk to and fro through the earth. And the man that stood among the myrtle-trees, answered and said, We have walked to and fro through the earth, and behold, all the earth sitteth still and is at rest. And the angel of Jehovah answered and said, Jehovah of hosts, how long wilt thou not have mercy on Jerusalem and on the cities of Judah, against which thou hast had indignation these seventy years? And Jehovah answered the angel that talked with me good words, comforting words. And the angel that talked with me said unto me, Cry, saying, Thus saith Jehovah of hosts: I am jealous for Jerusalem and for Zion with a great jealousy, and I am wroth exceedingly with the nations that are at ease; for I was but a little wroth, and they helped forward the affliction. Therefore thus saith Jehovah: I am returned to Jerusalem with mercies: my house shall be built in it, saith Jehovah of hosts, and the line shall be stretched forth upon Jerusalem. Cry further, saying, Thus saith Jehovah of hosts: My cities shall yet overflow with prosperity, and Jehovah shall yet comfort Zion, and shall yet choose Jerusalem.

Altogether, there are eight visions recorded that Zechariah saw. In one night, the word of the Lord came to him, and he continuously saw eight different visions. All these visions were consecutive—one added to the other. Combined together, they give us the whole picture of how the Lord was going to gain glory out of His people. The first vision which Zechariah saw in the night had to do with the Lord's jealousy.

Upon the four and twentieth day of the eleventh month

Zechariah's prophesying began with a call for the remnant of the children of Israel to return to Him in their hearts. They had already returned physically, but their hearts needed to be recovered. This call was spoken in the eighth month, in the second year of King Darius. Then, in the eleventh month of that same "second year of Darius came the word of Jehovah unto Zechariah the prophet" again.

Remember that after Zechariah prophesied in the eighth month, Haggai prophesied again in the ninth month. That was a turning point for the remnant because Haggai prophesied that from that day onward, they would see the blessing of the Lord.

So evidently, after Zechariah prophesied for them to return, their conscience was again stirred up, and the builders returned to the Lord with their whole hearts. The result was that the Lord returned to them as well. About two months passed, and Zechariah prophesied again. This prophecy was a long one.

he stood among the myrtle-trees that were in the low valley

> I saw by night, and behold, a man riding upon a red horse, and he stood among the myrtle-trees that were in the low valley; and behind him were red, bay, and white horses (Zechariah 1:8).

Zechariah saw a low valley full of myrtle trees. Some people think that this young man probably went to such a place often during the day. There may have been such a place like this low valley full of myrtle trees. As the young man Zechariah worked in the daytime, he may have gone into the valley among the myrtle trees to meditate, commune with God, pray, and pour out his heart before God. If he did that in the daytime, then in the night, as his mind was occupied in such a way, the vision would come. That might or might not be what happened, but we know that this was a vision given to him by God.

He saw myrtle trees in the low valley. Notice it was a valley and not a mountain. Notice that these were myrtle trees and not the cedars of Lebanon. When the Bible describes glory, the glory of the nature of Israel, the glory and the beauty of man, the Bible uses the cedar trees of Lebanon. (Many years ago, I went to Lebanon to see these cedars. They were majestic!) When the nation of Israel was in glory, they were like the cedars of Lebanon. But now, this little remnant determined they were as the myrtle trees in the low valley.

You know the Hebrew name of Esther is Hadassah, which means myrtle, as in myrtle tree. Myrtle trees are simple trees and smaller in comparison to others. They are lowly and usually grow beside the waterfalls.

The Bible uses the myrtle tree to describe the remnant of the nation of Israel before God. In the eyes of man, the remnant was small and lowly as the myrtle trees in the lowland. They were very low in the sight of man. Yet, from the supply of water—by the grace of God—they gave to God much fragrance.

the man that stood among the myrtle-trees … the angel of Jehovah answered and said

Then he saw a man standing in the midst of the myrtle trees. This man was called the Angel of Jehovah. In the Old Testament times, the phrase *the Angel of Jehovah* was special. He was not just one of the angelic beings. The Angel of Jehovah pointed to the second Person of the Trinity.

When Moses saw the burning bush in the wilderness, the Angel of the Lord was in the burning bush. In Zechariah, a man was in the midst of the myrtle trees in the low valley. That Man was the Angel of the Lord. Think of that!

Though Israel at that time was in such a low state—government was taken away from them and given to the Gentiles—yet the Lord condescended himself to be in the midst of them. How comforting that was.

We are but earthen vessels, but there is a treasure in this earthen vessel (see II Corinthians 4:7). Who are we? We are nothing. In the eyes of man, we are nothing, and the church of God is nothing. Those who stand for the testimony of Jesus are as myrtle trees in the low valley in the eyes of man. They are weak, lowly, and humble. Yet it pleases the Lord to be in the midst of them:

> For where two or three are gathered together unto my name, there am I in the midst of them (Matthew 18:20).

It may not be a mountain top; it may not be such a statue that can be seen by the world. It may be hidden in the low valley as myrtle trees, but if anyone will answer even a little to God, there will be His presence. The Lord condescends himself to dwell among these lowly people.

behold, a man riding upon a red horse …
behind him were red, bay, and white horses

Then the vision continued. He saw a man riding a red horse coming, and behind that man, there were red, bay, and white horses. In other words, a team of horses. They came before this man who was in the midst of the myrtle trees. The prophet was curious, so he asked the interpreting angel who stood by:

what are these?

Many have tried to figure out what these horses are. Some believe they may be the four horsemen from Revelation 6 or Matthew 25. Red might represent war, for example. I do not know. But what we do know is this team of horsemen on their horses of different colors stood by the Lord going through the earth to bring back reports.

These are they whom Jehovah hath sent to walk to and fro through the earth (Zechariah 1:10b).

Such a concept was not strange in the Old Testament. In Genesis 18, God and two angels appeared to Abraham. After they finished their visit, Abraham walked with them for a distance to see them off. This is just like friends would do. You do not just say goodbye inside the house, but you go out your door and maybe walk a little bit with your friends. So Abraham walked with God and the two angels. And God said, "Can I keep away any secret from my friend

Abraham?" Do you remember what God said? He said, "Since the cry of Sodom and Gomorrah's sin is great, I will go down and investigate it. Of course, God knew everything. He did not need to investigate. He did not need to send someone out to come back with a report. But this is for our sake, that we may understand. So this concept of investigating what is happening on the earth is not strange in the Old Testament time.

God sent out this team of horsemen throughout the whole earth to see what was happening and to give a report to the Lord. The report was that the whole earth was at rest. During the time of King Darius, there was peace on the earth. There was calm and peace on this earth.

how long wilt thou not have mercy ...?

When the Angel of the Lord heard that report, you know what he did? The Angel of the Lord answered and said,

> Jehovah of hosts, how long wilt thou not have mercy on Jerusalem and on the cities of Judah, against which thou hast had indignation these seventy years? (Zechariah 1:12)

The whole earth was at rest, but this remnant was struggling restlessly in Jerusalem. Think of that! The whole earth was at rest, but those who really were in business with God had a very difficult time. Isn't that strange? Even today, it may seem strange to our eyes, but it is so often true. The world seems to prosper, the worldly people seem to be at peace, the worldly Christians seem to have a good time; but those who want to do the will of God—who have given up everything for the Lord—always seem to be struggling and having a difficult time.

Sometimes you wonder why. Why is it that those who do not know the Lord, or those who know the Lord but do not love the Lord, seem to have a very good time on this earth, but if you have some heart for the Lord, it seems as if the Lord gives you a very difficult time? Does that not make you a little bit angry? Does that sometimes stir up your flesh? Other people can. Why can't I? Why should I live in such a way? Does God really know?

Brothers and sisters, you do not need to ask for anything. Before you ask, Someone has already asked for you. The Angel of the Lord puts up that request. When the Angel of the Lord heard the report, He turned and said, "Oh, Jehovah of hosts"—the Son is praying to the Father. Our Lord Jesus is acting as the Intercessor.

Oh, brothers and sisters, our Lord Jesus is in the midst of His people, and as His people go through afflictions, He is equally afflicted! He will take up our cause. He will plead with the Father. He is our great High Priest.

Even when He was on earth, how He prayed for Peter, "Simon, Simon, Satan wants to lay his hand on you to sift you, but I have prayed for you. After you have returned, strengthen your brethren" (see Luke 22:31).

And now He is at the right hand of the Father. Sleeping? No. Interceding for us so that "he is able to save completely those who approach by him to God" (Hebrews 7:25).

Brothers and sisters, our Lord never sleeps nor slumbers (see Psalm 121:4). You do not need to feel envious of those in the world at all. Even before you ask, He answers. He is there at the right hand of the Father pleading our cause.

He turned to the Father and said, "Oh, Father, isn't that enough? These people who have suffered so much, seventy years of captivity. Isn't that long enough? Won't You do something? Will You return to them in mercy?" How can the Father refuse the prayer of the Son? The Bible says,

> And Jehovah answered the angel that talked with me good words, comforting words (Zechariah 1:13).

Immediately, the answer of the Lord came, and the angel who interpreted said to Zechariah good words, comforting words.

I am jealous for Jerusalem and for Zion with a great jealousy

What were the words that were so comforting? God has been jealous for Jerusalem and for Zion.

And the angel that talked with me said unto me, Cry, saying, Thus saith Jehovah of hosts: I am jealous for Jerusalem and for Zion with a great jealousy (v. 14).

In the original language, it says, "I *have been* jealous" instead of "I *am* jealous." In other words, God did not begin to be jealous right at that time. He had been jealous all along. "I have been jealous for Jerusalem and for Zion with a great jealousy." Do you know that our God is a jealous God?

Sometimes words have an unwarranted bad connotation. There is nothing wrong with jealousy in itself. Even to hate, in itself, is not wrong. If we do not know how to hate, then we have no character at all. We may think love is good, but hate is bad. No, love and hate can both be good and bad. If you love what you should not love, that is bad. If you hate what you should hate, that is good. It is the same with jealousy. It is just an emotional expression.

When God gave the Ten Commandments to the children of Israel, He said,

For thou shalt worship no other God; for Jehovah—Jealous is his name—is a jealous God (Exodus 34:14).

Even His name is Jealous. That is His name. Our God is so jealous that He is a consuming fire:

> For Jehovah thy God is a consuming fire, a jealous God (Deuteronomy 4:24).

Our God is a jealous God. Jealous for whom? The Lord said, "I have been jealous for Jerusalem and for Zion with a great jealousy."

You are not jealous for anything that you do not value very much. Let people take it away. Let people have those things that you do not value. They are nothing to you. But if something is very dear to you, then you watch it with jealousy:

> For love is strong as death; Jealousy is cruel as Sheol: The flashes thereof are flashes of fire, Flames of Jah (Song of Songs 8:6b).

In II Corinthians 11, Paul said, "I am jealous as to you with the jealousy of God" Why? "Because I have espoused you to one Man, that is Christ. I presented you as chaste virgins to that Man, and I am jealous lest you be enticed ..." (see vv. 2-3a).

Why was Jerusalem destroyed? Why was the temple destroyed? Why were there seventy years of captivity? Why? Was it because God did not love His people? No. It was because God was jealous for Jerusalem and Zion. When Jerusalem and Zion did not meet His heart, they had to be disciplined, even destroyed for a time so they might return to God. That was the reason.

and I am wroth exceedingly with the nations that are at ease; for I was but a little wroth, and they helped forward the affliction (Zechariah 1:15).

God was jealous over Jerusalem and Zion, and because of that jealousy, God allowed His people to be taken into captivity as a chastisement. But unfortunately, the rod that God raised up for the chastisement of His people lifted up himself and said, "Ah-ha! This is my opportunity!" They "helped forward the affliction" of God. God only wanted to chastise His people, to bring His people back. God used the nations to accomplish that purpose. But the nations did not know God, and they went forward beyond God's "little wrath," oppressing His people to the extreme. God said, "I am angry with these nations. They did too much. They did far more than I purposed them to do."

Oh, brothers and sisters, is this not true today? Oftentimes, the world goes beyond what God wants them to do. They go too far in afflicting us. God said,

I am returned to Jerusalem with mercies

The Lord is still jealous, so He will return "to Jerusalem with mercies." The same God who was jealous to allow His people to be taken into captivity was now also jealous to return to His people with mercy. He said,

> my house shall be built in it, saith Jehovah of
> hosts, and the line shall be stretched forth upon
> Jerusalem. Cry further, saying, Thus saith
> Jehovah of hosts: My cities shall yet overflow
> with prosperity, and Jehovah shall yet comfort
> Zion, and shall yet choose Jerusalem (Zechariah
> 1:16b-17).

Oh, thank God for that! God was comforting His people. Understand the hand of the Lord. If you understand, if you submit yourselves to the mighty hand of God, in due time, He will exalt you (see I Peter 5:6). He will comfort you.

Oh, brothers and sisters, if only we know how God is jealous for those whom He has set His heart upon, then we will understand what He is doing. We will not misunderstand Him. He chastens those whom He loves (see Hebrews 12:6). He disciplines us so that we may be partakers of His divine will. And if we learn to submit ourselves under His mighty hand, He will return to us with gladness (see Jeremiah 31:13). He will build us together. He will yet choose us.

The prophet Zechariah was comforted and was able to use these words to comfort the remnant who were struggling with difficulties.

So dear brothers and sisters, in this first vision, Zechariah saw something very precious. Never judge anything by its outward appearance. The outward appearance can be very deceiving. Instead, go to the Lord about it. If the Lord should open your eyes, you will see how merciful He is, how good He is. Oh, may the Lord strengthen our faith.

Lord, Thou dost comfort Thy people. Lord, Thou dost choose to dwell with Thy people in their lowliness. Thou dost take up their cause and intercede for them. Thou art jealous for Thy people. Thou wilt see to it that Thy cities be inhabited, and Thy house be built. Oh, how we praise and thank Thee! It is all Thy doing. We only pray that we may not be those who have a veil upon our hearts who cannot see. Oh Lord, make us see that we may worship Thee. Amen.

4—The Second Vision: Gathering

Zechariah 1:18-21—And I lifted up mine eyes, and saw, and behold four horns. And I said unto the angel that talked with me, What are these? And he said to me, These are the horns which have scattered Judah, Israel, and Jerusalem. And Jehovah shewed me four craftsmen. And I said, What come these to do? And he spoke, saying, Those are the horns which scattered Judah, so that no man lifted up his head; but these are come to affright them, to cast out the horns of the nations, which lifted up the horn against the land of Judah to scatter it.

There are eight visions altogether that Zechariah saw in one night continuously. Through these visions, we can see the whole plan of God in the work of recovery. God will recover His people fully in the end. We will concentrate more on just a few of these visions—the first, fourth, and fifth visions. But I will mention a little bit about the second and third visions so we may see how they are each added to the other. First, let us remember the situation with the remnant and the prophets.

For the sake of the rebuilding of the temple, God raised up prophets to confirm and strengthen the word of the Lord to the remnant. He not only raised up an old man, Haggai, to be his spokesman, but also a young man, Zechariah. When Zechariah began to prophesy, there was a message of the Lord to the remnant:

> Return unto me, saith Jehovah of hosts, and I will return unto you, saith Jehovah of hosts (1:3b).

Though the remnant at that time were already stirred by the Spirit of God to build the temple, God's word to them was still, "Return unto Me, and I will return unto thee." God was interested in their hearts more than in their position or work. Positionally, they were already in Jerusalem. And so far as the work was concerned, their hands were already working on the temple. But God said, "How about your heart? Is your heart pure?" A pure heart was the only thing that could satisfy God. So even to the remnant who were in the right place, doing the right thing, God's word was, "Return unto Me, and I will return unto thee." And thank God, they did return.

And because of that, in the eleventh month, Zechariah prophesied again after seeing eight visions in one night.

> I saw by night, and behold, a man riding upon a red horse, and he stood among the myrtle-trees that were in the low valley; and behind him were red, bay, and white horses (Zechariah 1:8).

In the first vision that Zechariah saw, he was in a low valley full of myrtle trees. Myrtle trees are lowly trees that grow in the valley near the water. So far as the remnant who returned to Jerusalem was concerned, they were no longer in a position of strength and glory like the cedars of Lebanon. Though they were in the low valley, they still drew water—the grace of God—and they were very fragrant before God as myrtle trees.

Also, in that first vision, the Angel of the Lord was in the midst of the myrtle trees. In other words, the Lord condescended himself to be with His people who were in such a low state. The Lord did not leave them nor forsake them. The Lord was with them.

He also saw a man riding a red horse, and behind him were red, bay, and white horses—a team of horsemen. These were the messengers sent out by God to search throughout the whole earth and report to Him what was happening. They reported to the Angel of the Lord—the second Person of the Trinity—that the whole world was at peace. This was during the reign of King Darius, and at that time, the whole earth was at rest.

But while the whole earth was at rest, God's people were struggling. The world may be at rest, yet those who want the Lord seem to have great difficulties. They may wonder why. The answer from the Lord is that our God is a jealous God. He is not jealous over things or people that He has no interest in. He is jealous over Jerusalem and over Zion because He loves Jerusalem and Zion so much. Since He loves so much, He is so jealous. He deals with them strictly. He disciplines them in order to bring them back to himself fully and perfectly.

This explains the discipline that God's people go through. But God also says that He will return with mercy. In the end, He will bless them. That is the first vision.

After the first vision passed, Zechariah lifted up his eyes and saw a second vision.

and behold four horns

Horns in the Scripture always represent power. Here he saw these four powers. He asked, "What are these?"

These are the horns which have scattered Judah, Israel, and Jerusalem

These four powers of the world had scattered the nation of Israel. The world uses its power to scatter God's people. That is what happened to the nation of Israel. These four powers in this vision are the same as the four world empires that Nebuchadnezzar had seen (see Daniel 2). The nation of Israel had been scattered, but that was not the end.

And Jehovah shewed me four craftsmen

God chose four craftsmen who would break these horns. In other words, through these craftsmen, the nation of Israel shall be regathered together, and that is what God promises and what God is doing.

Brothers and sisters, the powers of this world always try to scatter God's people lest they be united and become strong. But thank God, He has His craftsmen;

He has His way of dealing with the powers of this world to bring His people together as a testimony to His name.

5—The Third Vision: God's Presence

Zechariah 2:1-13—And I lifted up mine eyes, and saw, and behold a man with a measuring line in his hand. And I said, Whither goest thou? And he said unto me, To measure Jerusalem, to see what is the breadth thereof, and what is the length thereof. And behold, the angel that talked with me went forth; and another angel went forth to meet him, and said unto him, Run, speak to this young man, saying, Jerusalem shall be inhabited as towns without walls for the multitude of men and cattle therein; and I, saith Jehovah, I will be unto her a wall of fire round about, and will be the glory in the midst of her. Ho, ho! flee from the land of the north, saith Jehovah; for I have scattered you abroad as the four winds of the heavens, saith Jehovah. Ho! escape, Zion, that dwellest with the daughter of Babylon. For thus saith Jehovah of hosts: After the glory, hath he sent me unto the nations that made you a spoil; for he that toucheth you toucheth the apple of his eye. For behold, I will shake my hand upon them, and they shall become a spoil to those that served them: and ye shall know that Jehovah of hosts hath sent me.

Sing aloud and rejoice, daughter of Zion; for behold, I come, and I will dwell in the midst of thee, saith Jehovah. And many nations shall join themselves to Jehovah in that day, and shall be unto me for a people; and I will dwell in the midst of thee, and thou shalt know that Jehovah of hosts hath sent me unto thee. And Jehovah shall inherit Judah as his portion in the holy land, and shall yet choose Jerusalem. Let all flesh be silent before Jehovah; for he is risen up out of his holy habitation.

The eight consecutive visions that Zechariah saw in one night each build upon the other. Through these visions combined we can see the whole plan of God in the work of recovery. Based on the first and second visions, Zechariah now saw the third vision.

behold a man
with a measuring line in his hand

Whenever a man has a measuring line, you know that something is being built and needs to be measured to see whether it meets the standard of God. God was building His city, and the man was to measure the width and length of Jerusalem. But it will be of such dynamic dimensions.

Jerusalem shall be inhabited
as towns without walls

Jerusalem will have so many people that it will be a city without walls. If you have walls, you are limited. But here, God is building the city of Jerusalem for the inhabitants, and He builds it even without walls. There will be such length and breadth that it cannot be measured. Does this mean there are no walls there? There is a wall. God said,

I will be unto her a wall of fire round about, and will be the glory in the midst of her

The blessing of the Lord was such that it was unlimited. But God was the wall of fire. God protected them. And God was the glory in their midst.

Then there were specific words for three different kinds of people.

Ho! escape, Zion, that dwellest with the daughter of Babylon

First, to those who still lived in Babylon, God's word was, "Flee! Come out of it!" God was going to punish Babylon, and if His people remained, they would suffer loss. So the Lord spoke to His people who still remained in Babylon, "Flee Babylon!"

rejoice, daughter of Zion for behold, I come, and I will dwell in the midst of thee

Then there were the words to the daughter of Zion, those people who had already come out of Babylon and returned to Jerusalem. They were the daughter of Zion. God's word to them was, "I will dwell with you. I will be a wall of fire around you and the glory in your midst." These were comforting words.

Let all flesh be silent before Jehovah for he is risen up out of his holy habitation

Then God had a word for all flesh, for the whole world. The word of God was, "Let all flesh be silent." God has started to work—"he is risen up"—so let all flesh be silent.

Brothers and sisters, the Spirit's application is as real today as it was with the children of Israel at that time. What is God's word to those believers who still dwell in Babylon—in spiritual confusion? His word is "Come out of her" (see Revelation 18:4). The time is coming when God is going to avenge His Son.

And to those who are daughters of Zion, the word of the Lord is, "I am in your midst" (see Matthew 18:20). No matter how difficult it is, He is in their midst. He is a wall of fire around them and the glory within.

And to all flesh, all the people of the world, God says to be silent. God has risen up out of His holy habitation. He is working. Be careful.

6—The Fourth Vision: the Priesthood

Zechariah 3:1-10—And he shewed me Joshua the high priest standing before the Angel of Jehovah, and Satan standing at his right hand to resist him.

And Jehovah said unto Satan, Jehovah rebuke thee, O Satan! Yea, Jehovah that hath chosen Jerusalem rebuke thee! Is this not a brand plucked out of the fire? And Joshua was clothed with filthy garments, and stood before the Angel. And he spoke and said unto those that stood before him, saying, Take away the filthy garments from off him. And unto him he said, See, I have caused thine iniquity to pass from thee, and I clothe thee with festival-robes. And I said, Let them set a pure turban upon his head. And they set the pure turban upon his head, and clothed him with garments; and the Angel of Jehovah stood by.

And the Angel of Jehovah protested unto Joshua, saying, Thus saith Jehovah of hosts: If thou wilt walk in my ways, and if thou wilt keep my charge, then thou shalt also judge my house, and shalt also keep my courts; and I will give thee a place to walk among these that stand by.

Hear now, Joshua the high priest, thou and thy fellows that sit before thee—for they are men of portent—for behold, I will bring forth my servant the Branch. For behold, the stone that I have laid

before Joshua—upon one stone are seven eyes;
behold, I will engrave the graving thereof, saith
Jehovah of hosts, and I will remove the iniquity of
this land in one day. In that day, saith Jehovah of
hosts, shall ye invite every man his neighbour
under the vine and under the fig-tree.

The remnant came back under the leadership of
Zerubbabel and Joshua. Zerubbabel was of the royal
seed of David, and Joshua was of the seed of Aaron. He
was the high priest. So under the joint leadership of the
king and the priest, the remnant came back to Jerusalem
to rebuild the temple—the testimony of God on earth.
Here both the kingship and priesthood are represented
through Zerubbabel and Joshua.

And he shewed me Joshua the high priest standing before the Angel of Jehovah

As the high priest, Joshua had the breastplate upon
his breast with the names of the twelve tribes of Israel
inscribed on twelve precious stones. He also had the
names of the twelve tribes inscribed on onyx stones on
his shoulders. So when he entered into the Holy of
Holies, he entered representing the twelve tribes of
Israel. The high priest represented the spiritual
condition of the whole nation and was responsible for
their spiritual condition.

In the recovery of the testimony of God, one thing
must be recovered—the priesthood. The priesthood is
closely related to the spiritual state of all God's people

since it is through the priesthood that they are presented before God.

he shewed me … Satan standing at his right hand to resist him

Joshua must have been an old man at the time of Zechariah's vision. Joshua was standing before the Angel of the Lord. That was his position since the high priest was supposed to stand before the presence of God on behalf of all God's people, representing all His people. But Satan was also standing at his right hand to resist him. While Joshua was standing before the Angel of the Lord, Satan was standing at his right hand. Why? To resist him before the Angel of the Lord.

Satan is the accuser of the brethren, and we see an example of this in the case of Job. Satan appeared before God and falsely accused Job by saying, "No one really loves God. The reason why Job fears You is because You have put a hedge around him. You have blessed him so much. He really loves the blessing, not You at all. Suppose You take away all Your blessings, then we will see. He will curse You to Your face. There is no such thing as pure love towards God." Satan continued to accuse Job before God (see Job 1-2).

In Revelation 12, Satan is called "the accuser of the brethren" (v.10). How he accuses the brethren before God! Many times he accuses without ground. These are false accusations. Brothers and sisters, how often we suffer because of them. When Satan accuses us falsely, and we take it as if it is real, we will get into a poor condition. We will suffer for it.

But, sad to say, sometimes Satan accuses us with some legitimate ground. He does find some reason to attack. He finds some ground that he can use to accuse us before God. In those cases, even God cannot say, "There is no such weakness."

Satan never ceases to accuse. Whether it is true or false, he is the accuser of the brethren. Brothers and sisters, what shall we do when Satan is resisting us?

Toward the end of the earthly life of our Lord Jesus, He could say, "The ruler of this world has come, but there is no place for him in Me" (see John 14:30). This is our Lord. There is no place for the accuser in the life of our Lord Jesus. The Lord never gave any ground to the adversary. The adversary tried every means to get in, but he could not; there was no ground for him. On the contrary, our Lord Jesus defeated Satan on the cross so completely that He took him captive and made a public display of him on the cross (see Colossians 2:14-15). That is our Lord. But unfortunately, we are not as perfect. Unfortunately, we have many reasons for the enemy to accuse us. And along with these grounds, he accuses us even more by adding extra accusations.

And Joshua was clothed with filthy garments

Joshua was in a difficult position. Satan was standing by his right hand to resist him. It was as if the accuser was saying, "Who are you? Do you think you can come back to rebuild the temple? Do you think you can come back to serve God as a holy people? Do you think you can come back to restore the testimony of God? Look at yourself. You are clothed with filthy garments. You do not have the priestly garment at all. You are not qualified. How dare you! On what ground, what right, do you have to engage yourself in the recovery of the testimony of God? You are utterly incompetent. You are unworthy. You cannot do such a work. You are disqualified."

Joshua could not lift up his head. Why? Because he was clothed with filthy garments. How can any priest come to the temple with filthy garments? A priest who served in the temple would serve with *holy* garments, not *filthy* garments. They had priestly robes for beauty and ornament (see Exodus 28). When the priest presented himself before God, it was in such beauty, with such ornaments that were fit for serving in the presence of God. These are the garments needed to serve as priests. But here was Joshua, utterly unworthy, undeserving.

This was a terrible scene. If Satan should succeed in his accusations, then the recovery would suffer. There would be no priesthood. There would be no service. Even if the temple was built, the temple would be dead. Nobody should meet in that temple. Everything would be dead. It was a most critical time. But thank God, Joshua could not say a word. He himself could not lift up his head, yet there was One who spoke on his behalf.

Jehovah rebuke thee, O Satan! Yea, Jehovah that hath chosen Jerusalem rebuke thee!

When it says, "And Jehovah said unto Satan," this one speaking was the Angel of Jehovah. It was the Angel of Jehovah who was there. It was not Joshua, the accused, who answered the accuser. It was as if the judge answered the accuser on behalf of the accused. The Angel of the Lord was the judge, and he answered Satan the accuser, saying, "The LORD rebuke you, O Satan! The LORD who has chosen Jerusalem, rebuke you!"

The judge took the accuser to the side: "It is true that you have grounds to accuse Joshua, and Joshua has no way to answer you, but I can answer you." Why? Because the Lord had chosen Jerusalem. It was a matter of sovereign grace. Sovereign grace. Who is worthy to serve God? Who is worthy to be in the priesthood? No one. It is through the sovereign grace of God that all these will come to pass.

The Lord had chosen Jerusalem, and it was based on this election, His sovereign grace, that this rebuke came: "The LORD rebuke you!" It was not the accused who resisted the accuser, but the judge rebuked the accuser.

Is this not a brand plucked out of the fire?

Historically, the people in captivity were like wood in a fire. They would be completely consumed, but a remnant came back from captivity, like a brand taken out of the fire. The brand is already burned, scorched, and smoking. And if you snatch out something from the fire, you do not just snatch it out and then throw it back in the fire. You snatch it out because you want it. So God said, "I have snatched Joshua out as a brand out of a fire. I will not give him up. I will perfect him. I have a purpose in him. I will restore the priesthood so that he may serve in My house."

Oh, brothers and sisters, are we not also as brands plucked out of the fire? What do we deserve? We deserve nothing but eternal fire. We were sinners. We deserved death and eternal fire, but thank God, by His grace, He has plucked us out of the fire. It is true that we may be still smoking, but the Lord says, "I will not give up. It is My work. I am doing the work. I will perfect them. I will bring them to My purpose."

Is it not true that we are predestinated to be conformed to the image of God's Son? If there is a doctrine of predestination, here it is:

> Because whom he has foreknown, he has also predestinated to be conformed to the image of his Son, so that he should be the firstborn among many brethren. But whom he has predestinated, these also he has called; and whom he has called, these also he has justified; but whom he has justified, these also he has glorified (Romans 8:29-30).

We are predestinated to be conformed to the image of God's Son. We are the ones God has known beforehand. We are those whom God has chosen. We are those whom God has justified. And we are the ones He will glorify. Once He lays His hand upon someone, He will not give up. He will complete it. That is predestination. It is grace—sovereign grace.

God rebuked Satan, answering, "You may accuse him, but I am going to perfect him." He then spoke to those standing by, those ministering angels, and said,

Take away the filthy garments from off him …

Joshua could not take off the filthy garments himself. It was the Lord who commanded that the filthy garments should be taken away from him. In other words, it was grace.

> See, I have caused thine iniquity to pass from thee, and I clothe thee with festival-robes (Zechariah 3:4b).

Instead of those filthy garments, He had them put the festival robes on Joshua. These are the robes of the high priest when serving during the festival. In other words, with these robes, Joshua would be in his full glory. Now, you have to read Exodus 28 to see the full glory of the high priestly garments.

We need to keep in mind that this filthy garment that was upon Joshua and the festival robe that was later upon him is not the same as the "best robe" that the father clothed the prodigal son with when he returned in Luke 15. Here is something we have to understand.

When the prodigal returned to the father, he was a lad. So the father, after having forgiven his son, asked that the best robe be taken out and put on him. In this way, he might appear before the father in a worthy manner. That robe in the Scripture represents Christ as our righteousness. When we repent and come to God, He forgives our sin, and He clothes us with Christ. God has made Christ our righteousness so that when God looks at us, He sees the righteousness there. It is Christ, Christ our righteousness. And this robe can never be defiled. Remember that. Who can defile Christ? Christ is our righteousness. This righteousness always shines. It never changes its color no matter what you do. It is Christ. You may feel very low today, but your righteousness has not changed a bit. In other words, your position with God remains the same. You can come to God on the ground of Christ. You may change, but He never changes. That "best robe" cannot be defiled. It is Christ.

But there is another robe that can be defiled. We must be clothed with two garments, not just one. In Psalm 45, the queen was clothed with a garment of wrought gold, and over above that garment of wrought gold, there was a garment of embroidery. The garment of wrought gold represents Christ our righteousness which is the foundation of everything. The garment of embroidery represents the work of the Holy Spirit in our lives to produce Christ in us. This second robe is also found in Revelation 19, when the bride is shining in white linen garments, which are "the righteousnesses of the saints."

Not only do we have Christ as our righteousness, but Christ is wrought so much into our lives that it is like He is embroidered or knit into our lives, stitch by stitch. This is called the righteousnesses of the saints. It is still Christ, but it is the righteousnesses of the saints because it is wrought in us through the patient work of the Holy Spirit. This will be the festival robe, the holy garment that makes us fit to stand before God and serve Him.

Everything in that priestly garment is a virtue, the beauty of Christ. It is something that has been wrought into our lives by the Holy Spirit. This equips us to serve as priests before God. These are our festival robes.

But unfortunately, instead of having the priestly garment, Joshua's garment was defiled. He represented the spiritual condition of the remnant of the children of Israel. Though they had returned, how they are still worthless! They did not walk in the Spirit. There was much to be desired. And since it was not Christ manifested, but themselves who were manifested—their own feelings, desires, fears, concerns, interests, etc.— they were clothed in filthy garments. No one can serve God in such garments. Satan was right in that sense. He had the ground to accuse and resist. But thank God, the Lord had the filthy garment taken away. Joshua was washed in the blood.

In the book of Revelation, time and again, you find they wear white robes before God. Why? Because they were washed in the blood. It is not because they were perfect; they were not perfect. Brothers and sisters, we are not perfect. We are not better than anybody else. Oftentimes we fail, we fall, but we know the efficacy of the blood of our Lord Jesus. Oh, if we go to Him and have our robes washed in His blood, they will be white! Those robes are shining and pure.

So the filthy garment was taken away, and the festival robe was put on. We have our garments washed, and then the Holy Spirit begins to work Christ into us. He restores us.

Let them set a pure turban upon his head

Then something strange happened. After Joshua had put on the festive robe, we would think he was ready. But no, in Zechariah 3:5, we read:

> And I said, Let them set a pure turban upon his head. And they set the pure turban upon his head, and clothed him with garments; and the Angel of Jehovah stood by.

Oh, how he was in full sympathy with God, and the turban was put on! Now the high priest was completed. He was completely clothed and crowned, ready to serve in the temple. The priesthood was restored, and the Angel of the Lord stood by. In other words, He was the

One who made all these things possible. That was His answer to the accuser.

Brothers and sisters, in the recovery of the testimony of Jesus today, the spiritual condition of God's people must be restored. The holy priesthood must be restored. Does it not say in I Peter that we are "as living stones, are being built up a spiritual house, a holy priesthood, to offer spiritual sacrifices acceptable to God by Jesus Christ"? (v.5) On the one hand, we are living stones being built up together as a spiritual house, yes. But what will happen to that spiritual house if there is no holy priesthood? The house will be dead quiet, silent. There will be nothing going on, no sacrifice. The altar is there, but no sacrifice happens. The altar of incense is there, but no incense is burning. The table is there, but there is no shewbread to put on it. The candlestick is there, but no light is lit. What will happen in a house without the priesthood?

When the spiritual house is built, there will also always be a holy priesthood. We are all priests unto God. We are all to serve God. But how can we serve if we are clothed with filthy garments? That disqualifies us. Lots of God's people cannot function as priests before God. Why? Because they do not have the priestly garment to put on. All they are wearing are filthy garments. Oh, how we need to go to the Lord and ask for the washing with the blood! How we need to yield our lives to the Holy Spirit so that He may work Christ into our lives. As the character of Christ begins to form in us, we are able to function as priests. The holy priesthood must be recovered, and it is the Lord who does it all. It is grace. It only works if you let Him do it. He will answer Satan, the accuser of the brethren. He will bring back that holy priesthood, and there will be holiness unto the Lord.

If thou wilt walk in my ways ... I will give thee a place to walk among these that stand by

Joshua was clothed and crowned, ready to serve as the high priest in the temple that was to be built. Then the Angel of the Lord exhorted Joshua, protested even, saying, "Now that you are ready to serve, be faithful. Don't receive all this grace and mercy in vain. Now that you are washed, now that you have had the priestly garment put on you, now that by grace you are ready to serve—be faithful. If you are faithful, then you are complete in my house as a servant. You will be as those who stand by ready to serve."

So dear brothers and sisters, if we know the grace of the Lord in our lives, let us serve faithfully, according to the grace and the gift that God has given to us. This is what grace has made us for. This is what gift has been given to us for: that we may faithfully serve in His house. It is all so that we may be those who "stand by."

I will bring forth my servant the Branch

But God did not stop there. This recovery of the priesthood of Joshua was just a type. It was to be restored, but it was just a partial restoration no matter how much it was restored. The full restoration is in the future. The prophet prophesied now about the future days.

> Hear now, Joshua the high priest, thou and thy fellows that sit before thee—for they are men of portent [that is, types or symbols]—for behold, I will bring forth my servant the Branch (Zechariah 3:8).

"Here now" is said to Joshua, the high priest and his "fellows" who were "men of portent"—that is, men of type and symbols. "For behold, I will bring forth my servant the Branch." Joshua and his fellow priests, the holy priesthood, are just types of the One who is to come. God said, "One day I will bring in the Branch, My servant."

The concept of the Branch is not new to the Jewish people. Isaiah prophesied several hundred years before this:

> And there shall come forth a shoot out of the stock of Jesse, and a branch out of his roots shall be fruitful (11:1-2a).

There will be a shoot out of the stock of Jesse. Someone will come out of David, and the Branch out of those roots shall be fruitful. This Branch shall be fruitful. It is a tree, a vine with many branches. And the Spirit of Jehovah shall rest upon Him. In Jeremiah, you will find the same thing mentioned where God would bring in the Branch:

> Behold, the days come, saith Jehovah, when I will raise unto David a righteous Branch, who shall reign as king, and act wisely, and shall execute judgment and righteousness in the land (23:5).

God said, "I will bring forth my servant the Branch" (Zechariah 3:8b). The Branch is the servant of the Lord, that is, the Messiah or Christ. God will bring Christ in. And when Christ shall be brought in, what will happen?

behold, the stone

You know, in a vision, the scene can change very quickly. When God is speaking about the Branch, He may suddenly mention a stone. He said:

> For behold, the stone that I have laid before Joshua—upon one stone are seven eyes; behold, I will engrave the graving thereof, saith Jehovah of hosts, and I will remove the iniquity of this land in one day (Zechariah 3:10).

I wonder if the stone laid before Joshua, historically speaking, was the foundation stone they had already laid. The foundation stone of the temple was there before Joshua. But God used that stone to show Joshua that there will be a Stone not cut with the hands of man.

This Stone has seven eyes. Eyes in the Scripture always represent intelligence. This Stone is full of intelligence, having perfect wisdom and knowledge. Oh, the mind of God! The Stone is here to execute the mind of God.

In the book of Daniel, this Stone is shown to appear at the end. It will strike the golden image of Nebuchadnezzar so that it will be broken into pieces and disappear. This Stone shall become a mountain and fill the earth (see Daniel 2).

Oh, brothers and sisters, here you find the remnant had returned and were in such a low position. They were still under Persian rule. But God promised them that one day the ruling nations of this world, the powers of this world, would be broken up into pieces and disappear. The kingdom of Christ shall be established upon this earth, and God will do it.

He is building His kingdom. He said, "I will build My church upon this rock, and the gates of Hades shall not prevail against it" (see Matthew 16:18). And in Zechariah, He said, "I will remove the iniquity of this land in one day." This will literally be fulfilled when Christ comes back. At that time, He will remove the iniquity of the nations in one day. During the Millennial Kingdom, He will make Israel the head of the nations. They will be a nation of priests unto all the nations, as He had first ordained (see Exodus 19:6).

Spiritually speaking, is it not true already that Christ has put away our iniquity and made us enter into His rest? This is true even now with us.

In that day ... shall ye invite every man ... under the vine and under the fig-tree

Whenever the nation of Israel was at peace, under God's rest, they would sit under their fig tree and their vine and enjoy the Lord. This was always a picture in the Old Testament. Here they are described as inviting their neighbors to come. This means there is fellowship. Oh, how they had fellowship in the goodness of the Lord!

Dear brothers and sisters, our Stone is already here. Our Lord has taken away our iniquity. We are now resting in His goodness, and we can fellowship with one another. In the church, the priesthood is already fully restored. Oh, that God's people would be brought into fellowship with Christ and with one another! That is the fulfillment of the holy priesthood. Christ is the High Priest, and we are priests serving together under Him. In the restoration of the testimony of God, this priesthood must be restored. Thank God, He has promised to do it.

> Lord, do show us what mercy, what grace Thou hast bestowed upon us. How noble, how full are Thy thoughts concerning Thy people. How we praise and thank Thee that everything is grace, sovereign grace. Thou who hast begun, Thou wilt perfect it because Thou art faithful.
>
> So, Lord, we do look to Thee to restore the full priesthood in Thy church, that we may serve

Thee and one another, that we may fellowship with Thee and fellowship with one another. We ask in Thy precious name. Amen.

7—The Fifth Vision: the Kingship

Zechariah 4:1-14—And the angel that talked with me came again, and waked me, as a man that is wakened out of his sleep. And he said unto me, What seest thou? And I said, I see, and behold, a lamp-stand all of gold, with a bowl upon the top of it, and its seven lamps thereon, seven lamps and seven pipes to the lamps, which are upon the top thereof; and two olive-trees beside it, one on the right of the bowl, and the other on the left of it.

And I answered and spoke to the angel that talked with me, saying, What are these, my lord? And the angel that talked with me answered and said unto me, Knowest thou not what these are? And I said, No, my lord. And he answered and spoke unto me, saying, This is the word of Jehovah unto Zerubbabel, saying, Not by might, nor by power, but by my Spirit, saith Jehovah of hosts. Who art thou, O great mountain? Before Zerubbabel thou dost become a plain; and he shall bring forth the headstone with shoutings: Grace, grace unto it!

And the word of Jehovah came unto me, saying, The hands of Zerubbabel have laid the foundation of this house; and his hands shall finish it: and thou shalt know that Jehovah of hosts hath sent me unto you. For who hath despised the day of small things? Yea, they shall rejoice—even those seven—and shall see the plummet in the hand of Zerubbabel: these are the eyes of Jehovah, which run to and fro in the whole earth.

And I answered and said unto him, What are these two olive-trees on the right of the lamp-stand and on its left? And I answered the second time and said unto him, What are the two olive-branches which are beside the two golden tubes that empty the gold out of themselves? And he spoke to me, saying, Knowest thou not what these are? And I said, No, my lord. And he said, These are the two sons of oil, that stand before the Lord of the whole earth.

The word of God came to Zechariah in one busy night in a succession of eight visions, one after another. And in these eight visions, God made known to His people His whole plan of recovery. It was not just to recover the temple that Zerubbabel and Joshua and the remnant were building, but at the very end of days, He would recover everything to its fullest. So these eight consecutive visions lead us to the consummation of all of God's work of recovery.

In Zechariah 3, there is the vision of Joshua the high priest standing before the Angel of the Lord, as Satan stood by him to resist. In the recovery of God's testimony, there is one thing that must be recovered: the priesthood. What would the house of God be if there was no priesthood? Even after the temple was finished, if there were no priests to serve in the temple, then there would be no sacrifice or offering on the altar. There would be no water in the laver. There would be no light on the candlestick. There would be no shewbread on the golden table. There would be no incense burning on the altar of incense. There would be no service. There would be no praises unto God. Without the priesthood, the whole house would be silent. So in the recovery of the house of God, there must also be the recovery of the holy priesthood.

In the recovery of the testimony of God, not only must the priesthood be recovered, but the kingship must also be recovered. In the book of Revelation, we are told that the precious blood has washed us, and we have been made priests and kings unto God (see 1:5-6; 5:9-10). We are not only made priests unto God but we are also made kings unto God.

Joshua represented the priesthood because he was the high priest, a Levite. Zerubbabel represented kingship because he was a descendant of King David. At that time, Zerubbabel was in such a low place that he was not even independent as a ruler. He was *made* a governor by the Persian emperor. The royal seed of David should be on the throne of his father. There should be authority, there should be power, but here the royal seed of King David was made a governor of Judah by a Gentile king. Where was his power? Where was his authority? He had none. But thank God, God wanted to restore kingship to Zerubbabel.

This fifth vision—which is about the restoration of kingship—is especially related to Zerubbabel. Here we see how spiritual power, might, authority might be recovered so that we may be kings unto God, able to do things for God and accomplish His purpose.

It was King David who had the desire to build God a house. It was King Solomon who built the house. In other words, you need authority, and you need power to build the house of God. Kingship must be recovered.

And the angel … waked me, as a man that is wakened out of his sleep

After Zechariah had seen four visions, he went to sleep. Probably the visions were so great that he could not stand it. This is similar to the time when our Lord Jesus took Peter, John, and James to the Mount of Transfiguration. There our Lord was transfigured, full of glory. Moses and Elijah appeared and were talking with Jesus. These were important moments. How could anybody go to sleep? And yet the three disciples all went to sleep. These disciples just could not stand the glory of it. It was too much for the flesh. Now, if you were there, you would try to keep your eyes open. You would be just like a baby who does not want to fall asleep and tries to open its eyes but cannot help it.

Probably this young man Zechariah had a similar experience like that. After the four visions went by and the explanations were given to them, it all just overwhelmed him. It was just too much, and he went to sleep.

So the angel who interpreted everything woke him up. As if in a dream, he woke up, and the interpreting angel said, "Now Zechariah, what do you see?" There was more to come.

Dear brothers and sisters, thank God if He allows you to see something of Him, but remember that there is always more to come. Do not think that you have seen it all. As a young person, you may think, "I know it!" When the Lord begins to reveal something to your heart, you think to yourself, "I've got it all. There is nothing else. That's it." How often do we react that way! But don't leave God. There is more to come.

And he said unto me, What seest thou? ...
I see, and behold a lamp-stand all of gold

And then the angel that talked with him said, "What do you see?" And he said, "I see and behold …". Zechariah had spiritual eyes. He had spiritual insight. He said, "I see, and I behold …". Now, what did he see? He saw a golden lampstand, a lampstand all of gold.

Remember that Zechariah came from a priestly family. Though the temple was not yet finished—it was just in the beginning phase of building—as a priest, he must have been instructed in all the things in the temple and the services involved. So to a priest, a candlestick or a lampstand made all of gold was nothing strange. In the temple's holy place, there would be a lampstand made of gold. One of the duties of the priests was to light the lamp. So to see a lampstand all of gold was nothing strange to this young priest to be. He saw a lampstand all of gold.

a lamp-stand

We know what a lamp is, and we know what light is. The lampstand is that which uplifts the light. The lampstand itself does not have light. It is a vessel full of light.

And we know that the Lord Jesus is the light. In the Gospel according to John, we are told that John the Baptist is not the true light. He is just one who goes before, but the true light is the Son of God. The true light is the One who comes into this world and enlightens everyone (see 1:4-9).

The Lord Jesus said, "I am the light of the world; he that follows me shall not walk in darkness, but shall have the light of life" (John 8:12). He is the light of this world, and anyone who walks in that light will not stumble (see 11:9-10). In the city of the New Jerusalem, there is no need for the sun or the moon to give light. The glory of God gives it light, and the Lamb is its lamp (see Revelation 21:23).

The light is our Lord Jesus. He is the light. But this light needs to be lifted up so that it might shine forth. You do not put a light under a bushel (see Matthew 5:14-15). If you take a light and put it under a bushel, the light will be covered. Nor do you take a light and put it under your couch because all the light would be underneath it. Instead, you put a light on a lampstand so that it may shine for the whole house (see Luke 8:16). Christ is the light, but you do not hide Christ under a bushel.

A bushel is that which was used to measure wheat. In other words, a bushel represents the things and riches of this world. Do not let the things of this world so occupy your heart that the light of Christ is restricted.

A couch is where you take your rest. Do not allow the ease, comfort, and luxury of this life to take away the privilege of what we have been given. Christ must be put on the lampstand.

A lampstand, in the New Testament, represents the church. In Revelation chapters 1-3, the seven churches are represented by seven lampstands before God. Those seven local expressions of the church on this earth are seen as lampstands.

What is the meaning of the church? The meaning of the church is to uplift Christ. The church does not draw attention to herself; the church points people to Christ. The church is not the light; the church is the vessel for the light. Christ is the light, and the church is the lampstand.

all of gold

Now, in order to uplift Christ, there must be a spiritual capability given to us. That is why this lampstand is made of nothing but gold because gold speaks of the nature of God. There is nothing of man in it. It is all of God. This lampstand is made all of gold. Everything speaks of God's nature. It is God himself in man. It is of beaten work, a talent of gold being beaten into the shape and form of a lampstand (see Exodus 25:31; 37:17). God's light and nature in us must be wrought upon by the Holy Spirit through pressure. It is as if we are being beaten, beaten, and beaten. This beating is to mold us, shaping us according to the pattern of God.

with a bowl upon the top of it and its seven lamps thereon ... and seven pipes to the lamps

In this vision, we do not find a detailed description of the lampstand. Why? Because the people were familiar with it. When Moses was commanded to build the lampstand, God gave him a pattern on the mountain, saying, "Now watch. Do everything according to the pattern in the mount." In Exodus, descriptions were given of how this lampstand was built (see 25:31-40).

In the tabernacle of Moses, there was only one golden lampstand with seven branches. But when you come to the temple of Solomon, you find ten lampstands of gold. The one lampstand increased to ten. Then here with Zechariah, we are given another variation. It is the same lampstand but with a variation. The various lampstands in the Bible are basically the same, but there are variations to suit the needs or purpose of that moment. So this lampstand was not described in detail. It just says "a lamp-stand all of gold," but the prophet noticed something different from the concept that you had in the temple.

He saw a bowl or a reservoir at the top of the lampstand. The bowl was to store the oil there. I do not know if I picture it correctly, but probably this lampstand had only one shaft instead of seven. It probably went up in one shaft. And then there was a bowl on the top of the shaft. Then there were seven lamps on the bowl. So you find there is a little variation there.

Spiritual things are *never* dead and fixed. Spiritual principles are very living. They are suited to the special need of the moment, but basically, they are never changing. The prophet's attention was drawn to something different because that was the emphasis in the vision.

He saw the golden lampstand with a bowl for oil. And he saw seven lamps and seven pipes leading from the bowl to the lamps. In the original language, it is hard to decide whether it is talking about seven golden pipes leading from the bowl to the seven lamps or seven pipes for each lamp. If the seven pipes lead to one lamp, then you have forty-nine pipes.

and two olive-trees beside it, one on the right of the bowl, and the other on the left of it

And he saw two olive trees standing on the right and the left of the bowl. It was taken for granted that the golden lampstand was built according to the heavenly pattern. The emphasis in this vision was on how the light was supplied. It was all on the matter of oil. The bowl was for the storage of oil, the pipes were to transport and could channel the oil, the lamps were to use the oil for the light, and the olive trees were to supply the oil to the bowl. The whole emphasis is on the supply of oil. How was the light supplied? That was the whole emphasis. In other words, the vision's emphasis was not on the structure. The emphasis was on the utility.

What are these, my lord?

When Zechariah, the young man, saw this vision, he could not understand. He knew about the golden lampstand; he was familiar with that. But when he saw this golden lampstand with a bowl and pipes and the two olive trees, he could not understand. So he asked that interpreting angel, "What are these? What do they mean? What is the meaning of this vision?" And the word of the Lord came to him.

Before we go into the details of this vision, let us first get hold of the message, the word of the vision. Now that is most important. Why did God show Zechariah this vision? When you consider the vision as a whole, what message did God try to convey to His servant? What was the word of God? The word of God was,

Not by might, nor by power, but by my Spirit, saith Jehovah of hosts

That was the message. Can you make any connection between the vision seen and this word given? It is not enough just to see a vision. If you see a vision and you do not get a message, then the vision will soon fade away. When God gives a vision, you should receive a message with it. What is the message of this vision? The message is, "Not by might, nor by power, but by My Spirit." This message was especially to Zerubbabel.

Zerubbabel was leading the people in the building work of the temple. But as he was building the temple, he must have suffered much inwardly. Why? Because the rebuilding of the temple was a gigantic job for this small number of the remnant. It was a big job. It was not only a big job but they were also surrounded by enemies who were trying to frustrate and stop them. These enemies were resisting and trying to hinder them.

Besides the tremendous job and the enemies surrounding them, Zerubbabel also had neither might nor power. Why? He was *made* a governor of Judah by the Persian emperor. In other words, he had to look up to the Persian emperor for his favor. Zerubbabel himself had no influence, no power, and no ability. Everything in that area was lacking. There was no authority. How could a person without might, without power, finish this great work?

And more than that, the rebuilding of the temple was but a symbol. Why? The rebuilding of the temple was to restore the testimony of God on this earth. How could the light of God shine out to the nations, to the world? It was a job that was beyond imagination. And no doubt Zerubbabel must have been weighed down by the heaviness of the task.

When he thought of the task before him—to restore the name of God on earth, to restore the testimony of God on earth with only a handful of people, limited resources, under great difficulties, having no might, no power—Zerubbabel must have been troubled all the time. How could it be done? It cannot be done. It was beyond human possibility. It was impossible.

Was he looking for might? Looking for some connection with the Persian Court? Was he looking for power? Human power that he can rely upon? No. God said, "Not by might, nor by power."

Do not be disturbed because you do not have might. Do not be troubled because you have no power. Even if you have might and power, you do not help; you hinder. God is not looking for might in you. God is not looking for power in you. If you do not have might, if you do not have power, do not cry over it as if you lack something. You provide God with a right opportunity.

How often our human might and human power interfere with God's work! We think we can do it. We think we have the strength to do it. We think we have the wisdom, the cleverness to do it. We think we have the energy and ability to do it. And we just go ahead to help God. But the more we help Him, the worse it gets.

Who art thou, O great mountain? before Zerubbabel [thou dost become] a plain

Zerubbabel was faced with a tremendous job, that of building the temple. This meant the restoration of the light of the testimony of God. The task was difficult. A mountain of difficulties seemed to stand before him. How could the mountain be removed? How could it become a plain? Where was the power or the might to accomplish such a gigantic work? It seemed almost impossible to undertake such a work. But by the Spirit of God, that mountain would be "cast into the sea" (see Matthew 21:21) and become a plain before Zerubbabel.

God is the God of the impossible. The power and the might of the Holy Spirit is *limitless*. There is nothing too hard for God, nothing too hard for God.

and he shall bring forth the head-stone with shoutings: Grace, grace unto it!

God said, "Zerubbabel, whose hand has laid the foundation of the temple, he will finish it. And the day will come when the topstone will be put on it. Then they will shout and say, 'Grace, grace, unto it!'" That is the message of the vision. The whole emphasis of the vision is on how the testimony of God is to be maintained. How can light shine? Where is the supply? How is it to be supplied? Who is the supplier? The answer is: the

Spirit of God. It is not man that will do this. It is all by the Spirit of God.

Oh, if only we trust God! If only we trust the Spirit of God. The emptier we are, the more we will be filled. The less might and power we have, the more the Spirit of God will manifest His might and His power. The mountain shall be leveled into a plain. The house shall be finished. And remember, it is grace—"Grace, grace unto it!" If it is the Spirit of God, then it is grace because it is not you. It is all grace. God will do it.

The word of God came again to strengthen and encourage Zerubbabel, saying:

who hath despised the day of small things?

Thank God that it is "not by might, nor by power but by [His] Spirit." Zerubbabel had the Spirit of God, and that was all he needed for the building of the house, and yet Zerubbabel could not help but see how small this temple would be. Even if the house should be finished, he could see that this house would be very small compared to the temple built by Solomon. It would seem almost to be nothing.

Why didn't God do something big? Of course, God could. In rebuilding the temple, He could help the remnant build it even bigger than the temple built by Solomon. God could do that. But God didn't. The temple that came out of the hands of the remnant was a small one. Zerubbabel would probably think, "Well, what is this? It is nothing. If it is this small, how can the testimony of God be restored? It should be something big and majestic, and then the whole world would be surprised. But this little thing, what's the use of it? Will it restore the testimony of God on earth?" So God said, "Do not despise the day of small things."

There are days when God will do great things, but there are also days when God will only do small things. And if it is the day of small things, do not despise them. It is not a matter of whether it is big or small in the sight of man. It is a matter of where the eyes of God are. So the word of God said,

> ... Yea, they shall rejoice even those seven—and shall see the plummet in the hand of Zerubbabel: these are the eyes of Jehovah, which run to and fro in the whole earth (Zechariah 4:10).

Even in man's eyes, these are small things, yet the seven eyes of God that run to and fro through the whole earth focus upon the plummet in the hand of Zerubbabel. Oh, brothers and sisters, are we living in the day of small things? Are you looking for something big?

When a mustard seed grows, it becomes a vegetable plant, but in the Lord's parable, it unexpectedly became a big tree with all the birds of the air roosting upon it (see Matthew 13:31-32). We say, "Praise the Lord! the church now has influence in this world. The church has become a superpower." But who are these birds? They are the evil powers of the air. Brothers and sisters, God does not want us to be big on this earth.

When Christ was on the earth, He was called a Nazarene. People would say, "Does anything good come out of Nazareth?" He was despised. He was rejected. He was crucified on the cross. Do we expect to receive honor, glory, power, position, and dominion on this earth? This is the day of small things. Whenever anything gets bigger, and bigger, and bigger, be careful.

If we are faithful in little things today, God will give us greater in the kingdom (see Luke 16:10). Do not despise the day of small things. As long as the eyes of God are on them, that makes all the difference. If the eyes of the Lord are upon it, no matter how small it is, do it faithfully, as unto the Lord. In eternity, it will be revealed. If the eyes of the Lord are not on it, no matter how big or tremendous it is, it will be burned by fire.

In I Corinthians 3, we read about the fire burning our works. Some build on the foundation with gold, silver, and precious stones. Can you build something very big if you build with gold, silver, and precious stones? You cannot. They are too costly. But one day, at the judgment seat of Christ, fire shall appear. If the building materials are gold, silver, and precious stones, the fire will only purify them and add more luster. But if they are wood, grass, and hay, they will be burned. You yourself will be saved, but barely saved, as through the fire. Oh, you can build a big house with wood, grass, and hay! They do not cost too much. But they will all be burned. Do not despise the day of small things. The whole issue is: Are the eyes of God upon it?

You know, success is a great temptation. It is not success that measures everything. It is God's approval that measures everything. Do we seek success? Or do we seek God's approval? You may have success, but if you let me choose, by the grace of God, I will choose God's approval.

So Zerubbabel was *really* encouraged by this word: Do not despise the day of small things. Do not be discouraged, dear brothers and sisters. We live in the day of small things. Let us do what the Lord wants and do it under His eyes. That is all that matters. This is the general message of the vision.

... What are these two olive-trees on the right of the lamp-stand and on its left?
... What are the two olive-branches which are beside the two golden tubes that empty the gold out of themselves?

Then this young man Zechariah was rather curious. If you saw a vision like that with a bowl on the top of the golden lampstand having all these pipes, would you be curious? If the seven pipes lead to one lamp, then you have forty-nine pipes. Imagine seeing all those pipes there and then the two trees standing by. He was curious. Even though he received a message, he wanted to know more, so he asked the angel that talked to him and said, "Now wait a minute, before you go away, what do these two trees represent? Why are these two olive trees standing by?" And before the angel could answer him, he asked a second time. He was really curious. So he said again, "Now, what are these?" And he added something to it. He said, "Don't you notice something? These two olive branches that stand by the side of the bowl are pouring gold into the bowl." The olive trees were pouring out gold, and when the gold emptied into the bowl, it became the oil to go into the lamp. That's something strange. No wonder this young man wanted to know. So the angel explained to him and said,

These are the two sons of oil,
that stand before the Lord of the whole earth

Historically, the lampstand stands for Israel. Israel was the vessel to uplift the testimony of God. At that time, the two olive trees refer to Zerubbabel and Joshua. They would supply the oil. They were in spiritual responsibility for Israel. They would supply the nation with the power and strength of the Holy Spirit so that the testimony of God may shine. That is the meaning historically.

Spiritually, the lampstand represents the church. The church of God today is a lampstand all of gold. The church is called to be the vessel, the instrument, to uplift Christ so that the world may see and may believe in Him. That is the church.

But how is the oil supplied to the church? The oil is the Holy Spirit. The power and might of the Holy Spirit make it possible for Christ to shine forth. It is not by *your* might nor by *my* power but by *His* Spirit. So how is the might and power of the Holy Spirt supplied to the church?

Remember that these two "sons of oil" are olive trees. In the old days, they used olives for oil. Olive oil was not only for cooking but also for anointing and many things. The oil they used was olive oil. These two olive trees bear olives. For the olives to become oil, you have to crush them. The olives must be pressed and crushed until oil comes out.

Now let's look in Revelation 2 and 3 to find the two olive trees of the church. There we see seven golden lampstands before God, which are seven churches. Unfortunately, only one lampstand—the church in Philadelphia—has its light shining in full brilliance. The other lights are either flickering, smoking or dimming. The supply of oil is somewhat limited with these lampstands. The oil is running out, and because of that, these lampstands cannot uplift the light. In a sense, they cannot give the testimony of Jesus to the world. The Lord has revealed himself to these churches, and the churches cannot respond to the call of God to bear the testimony.

What does God do under such circumstances? In every letter to every church, He calls for overcomers. Here the church is lacking in the supply of oil. Now, who will be the vessel for the supply? The overcomers. God is calling overcomers in the church. They are the two olive trees supplying the oil. When the church seems to have failed in its responsibility and testimony,

God calls some in the church who will respond to Him with a perfect heart. They are like the olive trees that stand by the lampstand.

They are willing to be emptied first that they may be filled with the Spirit of God. They are the wise virgins who have extra oil. They not only have the oil in their lamps but also extra oil in the empty vessel. They become olive trees through the working of the Holy Spirit as the Holy Spirit controls their lives. They become olive trees that produce oil. Oh, brethren! How they need to be crushed so that the oil may flow forth!

This is what Paul was talking about in II Corinthians 4:

> But we have this treasure in earthen vessels, that the surpassingness of the power may be of God, and not from us: every way afflicted, but not straitened; seeing no apparent issue, but our way not entirely shut up; persecuted, but not abandoned; cast down, but not destroyed; always bearing about in the body the dying of Jesus, that the life also of Jesus may be manifested in our body; for we who live are always delivered unto death on account of Jesus, that the life also of Jesus may be manifested in our mortal flesh; so that death works in us, but life in you (vv. 7-12).

Brothers and sisters, are we willing to so dedicate our lives to the Lord? Are we willing to be in union with Christ in His life and presence? Are we willing to be emptied before Him so that we may be filled by the

Spirit of God? When we are filled with the Spirit, do you think we will have a good time? Do you think we will enjoy ourselves? Yes, on the one hand, there is great enjoyment, but on the other hand, there is the demand to pour forth as we are willing to be crushed.

Many of the difficult experiences of the higher kind are not because there is something in you that needs to be taken away. Some difficulties may be to help remove what is not pleasing to the Lord. But when you really enter into a deeper life with the Lord, you will find that God will lead you into crushing situations. You will be crushed, not because something is wrong, but because something needs to be given out to others.

Are you so selfish that you want to keep the Spirit to yourself? Do you want to be spiritual, filled with the Holy Spirit, and feel it, all for your own sake? He wants to fill you so that He may be poured out through you. Of course, the Holy Spirit himself will not leave you or forsake you. But when a person is filled with the Holy Spirit, he will have the Spirit of Christ. And just as Christ poured forth His life for the sake of the church, when you are filled, you also want to pour forth for the church. You pour oil into the bowl.

What did the two olive trees supply to the bowl? That which came out from the olive trees through the golden tubes was not oil but gold. When the Holy Spirit really controls your life, do you know what will come out? Gold. Gold is the life of Christ, the life of

God. One who is filled with the Holy Spirit will pour forth Christ.

The Holy Spirit does not want people to notice himself. He wants to glorify Christ. So when you are filled with the Holy Spirit, Christ is poured forth—gold. But when this gold goes into the lamp, it becomes oil—the Holy Spirit. The result will become life in the experience of other people. It is the Holy Spirit that convicts and convinces and becomes life.

These olive trees are pouring out all the time. The more they pour forth, the more they are filled. That is how the light is continuously maintained.

Brothers and sisters, today God is calling for over-comers in the church. "He that overcomes"—he who is willing to give himself completely to God. He is calling for those who will let the Holy Spirit control their lives so that they will have fellowship with His sufferings and be conformed to His death (see Philippians 3:10). Then the life of Christ will pour into the church, and the church will uplift Christ. Then the testimony of Jesus will be restored on this earth. This is the vision. This is the power. This is the authority. This is the kingship. We who have been washed by the precious blood have been made "kings and priests unto God." When you have kingship and priesthood restored, you have the testimony established.

Oh Lord, Thou dost encourage us. Thou dost show us Thy secret that it is not by might, nor by power, but by Thy Spirit. Oh, how we praise and thank Thee that Thou hast given to us Thy Spirit! This is the power of God. Oh Lord, teach us how to entrust ourselves to Thee and to Thy Spirit that we may not look to man, but we may cast ourselves upon Thee that the work may be done in Thy power.

Oh Lord, make us willing to pour forth for Thy church's sake. As Paul said that we may fill up the affliction of Christ for the church, His body. Oh Lord, that Thy church may truly fulfill her mission that the testimony of Jesus may shine forth. Lord, even though we may not see something spectacular, we want Your approval. Oh, if Your eyes are on us, Lord, we are satisfied. We are willing to be small, nothing. Lord, we want to follow Thee.

Oh, we commit ourselves to Thee, Lord, that Thou do something for eternity. We pray that our lives on earth may not be wasted but be fully in Thy will and purpose.

In the name of our Lord Jesus. Amen.

ORDER FROM: 11515 Allecingie Parkway Richmond, VA 23235
www.c-f-p.com

* 9 7 8 1 6 8 0 6 2 1 4 2 6 *